My Life Is a Road Atlas

THE HALIʻA ALOHA SERIES

My Life Is a Road Atlas

KATHY CLARKE

THE HALIʻA ALOHA SERIES

Darien Hsu Gee, Series Editor

Haliʻa Aloha ("cherished memories") by Legacy Isle Publishing is a guided memoir program developed in collaboration with series editor Darien Hsu Gee. The series celebrates moments big and small, harnessing the power of short forms to preserve the lived experiences of the storytellers. To become a Haliʻa Aloha author, please visit www.legacyislepublishing.net.

Legacy Isle Publishing is an imprint of Watermark Publishing, based in Honolulu, Hawaiʻi, and dedicated to "Telling Hawaiʻi's Stories" through memoirs, corporate biographies, family histories and other books.

Most of the names in this book have been changed to protect the privacy of the individuals involved.

ISBN 978-1-948011-69-3 (print)
ISBN 978-1-948011-70-9 (ebook)

Legacy Isle Publishing
1000 Bishop St., Ste. 806
Honolulu, HI 96813
Telephone 1-808-587-7766
Toll-free 1-866-900-BOOK
www.legacyislepublishing.net

Printed in the United States

For my mom

Ahead of her time,
strong and independent,
she taught me to be fearless.

CONTENTS

I KNOW OF NO HIGHER FORTITUDE THAN STUBBORNNESS IN THE FACE OF OVERWHELMING ODDS.

–LOUIS NIZER

When I was three and a half years old, I was shot point-blank with a .22 rifle. It was Price, Utah, December 1953, and I was sitting on the floor of our two-door Henry J sedan. The bullet tore eighteen holes in my abdomen and nicked my spine.

Dr. Whiting, who had served in WWII, knew all about gunshot wounds. He took me from my mother's arms, walked out the clinic door and held me as he drove the short distance to the hospital.

They said I would not live; if I did, I would never walk again. They said I would not have children. Later, they said I would not walk without braces.

Nobody told me.

When I was six, I took off my brace and refused to wear it. My mother said, "But, Honey, if you don't wear it, you will fall down."

I folded my arms, looked her in the eye and said, "Then I will fall down."

I never wore it again.

FOREWORD

My life is a story of determination, lived intentionally, taking on every challenge the world threw at me. For me, there was no other choice. When I was a young adult, I realized that no matter how sad, hurt or bad I felt, *I would always survive*. I look for the humor and enjoy the irony of everyday life. I hope my readers enjoy reading this book as much as I did living it.

I remind myself often: Kindness and compassion are a way of life, not a service dog.

STAYING ALIVE

I have never chosen the moments that defined me,
only how I faced them.

MAKING IT ALIVE TO TWENTY-FIVE

My parents didn't think I would live to be twenty-five. I really can't blame them. I sincerely believed that life was meant to be lived, having once almost lost it, and my mission was to make sure I lived every minute, however recklessly.

As a child, I was sassy and defiant, spoiled and fearless. No adventure was too great. No threat in the world would make me confess to eating all the grapes and spitting the seeds on the floor, nor stop me from climbing out my bedroom window, before dawn, to plaster honey on my brother and his friends during their backyard sleepover.

When the local bully targeted my older brother, Bert, my protective-sister-self took over. I was six years old and still wearing the leg brace and crutches. Having practiced on my older brother, I knew my crutch could do a good bit of damage in a wide, hard swing. The bully picked the fight and I finished it. His mother showed up at our door to give my father a piece of her mind. Dad knew my capabilities and called, "Kathy, get over here!" I hobbled my waif-like self up to the door on crutches, my metal brace clanking, wispy blond hair flying around my head like a halo. The woman took one look at me, turned to her son and said, "Is that the girl?" He nodded and glared hatefully at me. Looking at my dad, clearly embarrassed, she said, "I am so sorry to have bothered you, sir." She turned, grabbed her son by the ear and said, "You get yourself home right now. What were you thinking?" I looked on smugly as the boy's mouth fell open in surprise, then disbelief. "But, Mom, she—" She firmly marched him off. My father turned, looked down at me and scowled, barely suppressing a smile. "You know, you can't go around beating up little boys!" I stood my ground. "But he was being mean to Bert!" I exclaimed. My dad shook his head and walked away. I stalked to my room, not the least bit sorry.

I came by my rebellious ways naturally, as my maternal grandmother was a bit of a floozy. She was born on a farm in Idaho, one of nine children, six of them tall, buxom, healthy-looking Danish farm girls. Pictures of them show young women lined up in white shirtwaist dresses, frilled pinafores and sturdy black shoes with tortured hair in braids, buns and crimped waves across their foreheads. Their ankle-less, piano legs kept them firmly anchored to God's good earth. All except my grandmother.

The boys worked the land. The girls married farmers, railroad men and truckers. But Grandmother was having none of it. The first thing she did was change her name, from Katie to Katherine. She dropped her middle name, Elsina, like the rock it was. At twenty, she married Elmer in Salt Lake City, a long way from the Idaho farm.

Elmer knew he was a fine-looking man. A big, strong redhead, he and his brothers had been sent, as youngsters, to "work farms" when their mother died. The four brothers were later known to end a night of drinking by clearing out the entire bar, just because they could. Like their father, they never missed a horse race or turned down a shot of whiskey. Every woman loves a bad boy.

Elmer and Katherine loved each other their entire lives through a tumultuous young marriage, two children, hard times, a few marital affairs on both sides and long separations. Initially, they lived and worked on my great-grandfather's sawmill in the Utah mountains. They hunted deer for winter meat. My mother remembered her father leaving them once. Katherine angrily followed him to the city and came back with a black eye. Eventually, Elmer came home and they moved to a small coal mining town in Utah. Years passed. Their only son joined the Navy, my mom married my dad at sixteen and my older brother came eight months later. Katherine moved to Salt Lake City, lived in a basement apartment, worked at a bank and carried on with a married boyfriend. On weekends, she went dancing at the Saltair Ballroom but only danced with the young, good-looking men and scoffed at the old geezers her own age. As a child, while exploring her costume jewelry, I found a box with many different motel matchbooks in her drawer.

I asked what they were for. She smiled and said, "Just so I remember." Years later, I heard one of my cousins laughing about Grandma's "naughty" collection.

Elmer moved to Las Vegas in the early 1950s just as the US began testing atomic bombs in the desert. He joined the crews rebuilding the radioactive simulated towns and then, as a finish carpenter, he worked on many of the original casinos until he retired in the seventies. Katherine and Elmer remained married until 1962 when Katherine secured a divorce, intending to remarry. She backed out of that wedding at the last minute, but Elmer had already married his longtime live-in girlfriend.

When Elmer and Katherine were in their sixties, they started up again. Every summer, Elmer left his wife in Las Vegas, hauled his trailer to Salt Lake City, picked up Katherine and they went camping and fishing at one of their favorite lakes for weeks at a time. I guess true love never dies, it just gets put on hold sometimes.

CALIFORNIA BOUND

In 1954, Price was a small coal mining town in the middle of Utah. Its residents were highly opinionated and had a unique inability to mind their own business.

The town was well laid out, charming and utterly inbred. Everyone knew everyone else's business, and no one had any reservation about gossiping. Shriners Children's Hospital in Salt Lake City accepted me as a patient, and my parents were happy to make the move. They found a small house in the not-yet-labeled suburbs of Salt Lake and settled into a new life where your neighbor was not related to anyone in your family. I thought that house was a mansion until I went back to see it fifty-five years later. I was surprised at how small and tiny it was; basically a cracker box.

The house had three bedrooms, two baths, a carport and sat on a corner lot with a big front yard. On hot summer nights, our parents let us sleep on the front lawn. I remember wiggling excitedly, hugging my stuffed fur kitty and giggling at the stars. Bert would tell me to be quiet. On the Fourth of July, my father took the boys up on the roof to watch fireworks.

I was told I could not go up on the roof because I was a girl. I did not know at the time, but that was their standard excuse for anything physical they thought I could not do. Of course, I became a tomboy and wanted to do everything my brothers did. My mother wanted me to wear pretty dresses and I refused. The boys wore jeans and so did I.

When I was eight, my parents took a leap of faith and headed to California, the next stop in their Hawai'i dream. I remember in second grade, someone came to my class and escorted me to the principal's office. My father and brother, who was only a year and a half older than me, were waiting. The principal was talking and I could tell my dad was agitated as he took my hand protectively and my brother moved closer.

"You can't just take them out of school," said the principal. His tone was authoritative, his stance was intimidating. My father bristled. His shoulders shifted in anger, his jaw worked to one side and then back to clench in the center. My young father was not good with authority.

His eyes narrowed. "I can take my children out anytime I want." The principal drew himself up, obviously preparing for a confrontation. I was afraid.

"Where are you taking them?" challenged the belligerent principal.

My father's chin lifted defiantly. "We're moving to Hawai'i," he stated clearly.

We were going to Hawai'i?

My dad had been in the Navy and he never forgot his stopover in alluring Hawai'i. When we were babies, he sent a rayon aloha print shirt for my brother and a dress for me. I still have them.

I looked at my blond, freckled brother. No help there. I looked up at my dad. *Hawai'i?* I thought. The principal could not muster a response. Hawai'i wasn't even a state! My father took my brother's hand, turned and we walked out of school.

HOW TO PACK A CAR FOR A CROSS-COUNTRY MOVE

I will never forget packing up to leave Utah. My father limited us to what could fit in the car and he repeatedly asked if we *really needed that?* "Unnecessary" housewares were stored in our pink Buick and parked at an uncle's house for later retrieval. My mother put her foot down when it came to our clothes. She hated ironing (polyester had not yet been invented), so I learned how as soon as I could stand on a chair and lift an iron. She would dampen our clothes and Dad's dress shirts with a spray bottle, roll them up and place them in a plastic bag. When ironing time ran out, she put the bag in the freezer until the next marathon. The bulk of our wardrobe was frozen. The freezer held more icy rollups than ten-for-a-dollar potpies. She hung the crispy clothes out to dry and tossed them in the back seat, evidence of her housewifely guilt and defiance for all the other treasures she was forced to leave behind. We slept on that un-ironed pile all the way to California.

Limited quantities of essential linens, dishes, pots and pans were packed. A big cast iron dutch oven landed under the clothes. This pot was claimed by The Cat, who, of course, came along. Once on the road he prowled restlessly, cowered under the seats, burrowed into the monumental pile of ironing and, blissfully, found The Cast Iron Pot. It fit. The Cat curled up and went to sleep for three days. I don't think he peed more than twice on the whole journey. We held his leash on the roadside, but no amount of urging worked. He ate and drank little. Even a can of tuna or a vienna sausage would not lure him out of his pot. My brothers and I took turns lifting the clothes and peeking in to be sure he was still there. He gave no accusing or threatening looks. He purred, occasionally blinked, but never made a sound. He went limp and endured crushing hugs from my five-year-old brother, Kenny. He was stoic and he was our anchor.

The Cat was never grouchy like the parents in the front seat who kept telling us to "Leave the cat alone!" I remember Wonder Bread, Velveeta cheese slices, baloney and mayo sandwiches made on my mother's lap and passed over the seat. Ice cream was a bribe for peace and quiet.

FINDING WORK IN A STRANGE TOWN

My mother said we moved to California on a wing and prayer. We were all excited when we crossed the California state line, but it was still the same endless Nevada deserts. By the time we stopped in Las Vegas to see my grandfather Elmer, I had pneumonia. Grandpa and my mother took me to the doctor, and I remember he paid for it. We stayed a few days until I was better and we were on the road again. Dad got prickly when Grandpa expressed his opinion on my father's inability to take care of his family and his traipsing across the country.

We arrived in a new little Southern California town called Garden Grove full of vacant lots and new construction alongside fruit tree orchards. My dad, a printer by trade, bought a newspaper for the want ads. After a pay phone call, we drove to a local newspaper plant and we all waited in the car while Dad went in to apply for a job. He came out a while later and leaned in the driver side window.

"I got the job," he said. I felt my mother's relief as her shoulders dropped and her face relaxed

"But they want me to start right now."

"Right now?" my mother said, a little confused. "You mean *now*?"

"Yes, I know, but it's a job and they will pay me cash each day I work." My mom looked doubtful. If Dad went back in there to go to work, what were we going to do? My dad reached for his wallet and took out a fifty-dollar bill and held it toward my mother. I had a feeling it had come from my grandfather. "Here is my last fifty," he said to Mom. "Take this, find a place to stay. We passed some For Rent signs back a way. Here is the phone number of the paper. Call me and tell me where you are. You can pick me up when I get off work."

I can only imagine my mother's courage at that moment. She was all of twenty-six, Bert was nine, I was eight and Kenny was five years old. They didn't know a living soul in California, had no place to live, were out of money and were completely unfamiliar with the new, strange town. She slid over to the driver's seat and Dad gave her a kiss. He walked back inside and we drove away.

Somehow, she found and rented an unfurnished apartment. Daily? Weekly? How far could fifty dollars go even in 1959? The apartment had new carpeting so we were sure it was a very fancy place. We carried in the bedding, kitchenware and the monument to un-ironed clothes. Later that evening, Mom left us alone in this strange new place and went to pick up our dad.

We had The Cat, so we were just fine. We didn't know that Mom got lost and could not find the apartment she had rented. She and Dad drove around a long time before they found us. What a nightmare, to forget where you left your children! When they found us, we were sleeping in a heap on the floor with The Cat curled up between us. Sadly, the apartment didn't allow pets, and one day he was just gone. I cannot remember if we said goodbye or even if we knew he was going. We still had the pot and the ironing. Not a fair trade.

It was the end of March but Mom did not put us in school, as we were not there long. We played under a hot sun in a vacant lot next door. We were hungry sometimes but soon found a green weed that grew in the vacant lot that had a tight curled bud. They tasted nutty, so we ate them and something we called "sour grass." It was vaguely lemonish and we were impressed by this new state's abundance of natural foods. Our neighbors were diverse. The pretty lady, whose husband worked all the time, had the nicest furniture I had ever seen and a daughter my age. She let us play in the new baby's nursery and gave us homemade cookies and vegetable sticks. The boys who lived on the other side were grubby but very kind. Their parents spent all day and night in the bar down the streets so we had plenty of time to forage for food with them.

A month later, my dad heard of work in a union shop in Oakland. Before heading north, we visited the San Diego Zoo and made a short trip to Tijuana. Mom bought me a child-size, hand-tooled leather purse with a long shoulder strap. Dad bought the boys leather belts and coiled ceramic rattlesnakes.

MY FAMILY INVENTED LATCHKEY KIDS

It was May when we packed up and drove the coast highway north. In San Francisco, we visited Golden Gate Park and ate fresh shrimp at Fisherman's Wharf. We stopped by the *Oakland Tribune* to confirm Dad's job and then headed inland. The first No Vacancy sign we saw was in Lafayette at Morrell Manor Motel, where we lived in a two-room kitchenette for several months. Mom enrolled us in school and went to work for a bank. Bert escorted us to school, crossing a four-lane highway at the stoplight. We dropped Kenny at the adjacent preschool and I joined a class that laughed at me when I didn't know what month it was. Lafayette was a wealthy town and there is no doubt we were immediately labeled trailer park material.

During lunch recess, Bert, Kenny and I met in the corner of the chain-link fence where the two play yards intersected. The three of us just hung out there, sharing our peanut butter sandwiches, little fingers entwined through the fence.

When the bell rang, Bert and I left our baby brother clinging to the wire fence, watching until we were out of sight. His school day ended before ours and he crossed the same busy highway by himself. He waited for me on the motel stairs since I had the only room key safely tucked in my Tijuana purse. We didn't have TV, toys or games so when my older brother got home, we pulled out a deck of cards and played poker. We all knew four of a kind beat a full house and no matter how old the cards were, I could back shuffle. Sometime after dark, one of our parents would return. Homework was done and dinner was prepared. We didn't think any of this was unique, we just did what had to be done.

THE WILLOW TREE

After the motel apartment, we moved to a house in suburban Pleasant Hill. To me, the heart of the house was outside in the two weeping willow trees that filled (what seemed to be) a very large backyard. Everything good happened there. My new cat, who had appeared at Christmas, climbed the trees and took swats at the boys' heads as they ran by. The small pear tree gave up hard green fruit, always eaten before they were ripe. Birds nested in the treetop and the boys climbed high to watch them. I had to make do with their frustrating, less-than-descriptive responses to a repeated, "What are they doing now?"

The thick willow branches hung to the ground and created a green cave where running children could suddenly stand still and disappear. After a rain, we pulled on the branches and were in awe of the belated rainfall that soaked our laughing faces over and over.

Occasionally, Dad would trim all the hanging willow strands to a height just above our heads, hacking until it looked like a bowl haircut. Such an indignity for my beautiful willows.

My big tree stood solidly, cradled many young children and kept all their whispered secrets. It enfolded me in its swaying wands as I breathed the tree into my soul and let it wrap its green safety around me.

At night, it became a launching pad and anchored my tether when I learned astral flight. I wanted to leap into the heavens and fly around the world. Not to land anywhere, just to fly high and free in the perfect silence of the stars and the warm light of the moon.

I would sit on the roof until I was ready to leap into the vast night sky. I knew I was safe if I could still see the willow's huge, round head far below. When the silvery, white cord began to thin and I was tempted to seek freedom, the big willow tree gently pulled me back as his little sister nodded in approval of her guardian brother's responsibility.

ON BEING A DORK

My elementary and intermediate school years were spent in the willow tree house. When we left Utah, my rebel-self went dormant, leaving everything a monochrome of survival in a transient world.

In sixth grade, we had not yet been labeled popular or unpopular by our classmates but anyone "different" was always singled out. After a recent surgery, I was in a cast and on crutches, still painfully skinny, my long blond hair limp and straight with bangs above my glasses. A prime target, the mean boys called me "four legs and four eyes." Remembering my secret weapon used on the neighborhood bully, I patiently ignored their taunts, waiting until they came closer. In the play yard, circled by teasing boys, I carefully moved my right crutch behind me as far as I could, leaning on the left one. I coiled, waiting for an opening. When it came, I whipped my arm up and swung my crutch forward as hard as I could, aiming for a boy's head. I missed but gave his upper arm a solid whack. No one reacted so I launched a backswing and swiped another boy's shin. Both backed up, howling, as another predator backpedaled, then rushed forward. I had a crutch in his stomach before he knew what happened. A few kids cheered and laughed. Embarrassed to be bested by a girl, that was the end of their taunts and they gave me a wide berth. I was back.

The summer before my freshman year in high school, my parents bought a new home a few miles away, having given up their dream of Hawaiʻi. I was still skinny, had no breasts, no hips and needed a belt to hold up my skirt. I was officially a dork. In my junior year, I talked a doctor into prescribing prescription sunglasses. The dark lenses hid my eyes with oval frames that arched up and out at the sides. I wore them all day, every day. If I wasn't such a geek, I could have been cool.

In my creative writing class, I was the only girl in a select group of five guys, drawn together by our love of writing. We always sat together in the back corner of the room and often moved our desks to an inward facing circle to shut out the rest of the class. Our teacher hated me, presumably because I was the only girl in the creative boys' club. She was short, frumpy and used baby talk with the boys. She would give me a hall pass just to get me out of class and then refuse to give the boys any. My writing was creative and often unconventional, which she criticized relentlessly. The guys' loyalty knew no bounds and the more she ridiculed me, the more the circle tightened.

I had a crush on John Miller, who I later found out would not date me because of my bum leg. My best friend, Gary, had a crush on me. One day, Gary got so mad at our teacher for her treatment of me that he crawled behind the bookcase and curled into a fetal position. She cajoled repeatedly but he would not come out, so she kicked me out of class. Permanently. The principal made her let me back in. I did not get a good grade and she chose my worst piece of work for the literary magazine.

DODGING THE CHEERLEADER BULLET

Every group picture, in all my yearbooks, has me seated in the front row, like they thought I could not stand up with the rest of the kids. It was true, my leg sucked. The left one, skinny and useless for running, jumping, playing sports or dancing, still got me around in a gimpy kind of way and did not slow me down. It was just a fact, slightly inconvenient and generally irrelevant.

Years later, a roommate didn't notice for three months that I limped. In high school, it was all too obvious and it changed my life. If I hadn't had that lame leg, I am sure I would have been a cheerleader; blond ponytail, sassy, popular, and that would have led to an early pregnancy, marriage to some jock and probably fifty pounds of baby fat, never to be lost. Instead, my bum leg saved me. I was wildly independent and fearlessly determined to follow my adventurous path. Life turned out pretty good after all.

Once, while attending an industry conference, a self-important motivational speaker asked us to share. "What was the best and worst thing that happened to you this month?"

One moment please.

"Well," I said, "the best thing was going to my forty-fifth high school reunion." My table partners smiled expectantly, undoubtedly remembering their own happy reunions. "The worst was attending my high school reunion." I delivered it with a straight face and watched as faces wilted, looked confused and laughed nervously. Having killed the conversation, I reflected on my reunion classmates. The aging, frumpy cheerleader types still smirking, the potbellied, balding jocks still punching each other's shoulders. The demure ones remaining silent, never daring to offend, and the few truly nice classmates still being kind and friendly. No one had changed. No one had left town.

Except for one. I saw him sitting on his Harley. His long legs fit perfectly in Levi's, straight dark hair tied back, shadow beard, exceptionally handsome in his leathers and riding boots. My best friend, Gary, waved at him. "Who is that?" I asked. "Oh, that's John, you remember him?" I did. He had been a popular jock who never gave me the time of day. I rolled down my window, looked at him longingly and called, "Hey, John, will you marry me?" He looked startled. Gary gave him an apologetic look, rolled up my window and quickly drove off. Gary told me he was a preacher, married and living in the Northwest somewhere. He rode his bike down for the reunion. I was heartbroken. I loved motorcycles and this was certainly a regrettable, lost opportunity. Had I only known, I might have attended a reunion sooner.

AFTER HIGH SCHOOL

The summer after high school graduation, I met Bill. He was two years older, tall, lean, blond and blue-eyed with all the popular, cool kid credentials. Why he dated me, I never knew. Maybe it was the drugs he had been doing for a couple of years or maybe the antidepressants I later learned he was on. For our first date, I sewed a pink, daisy-print sundress. The shoulder straps and miniskirt hem were trimmed with lace daisies. Miniskirts were the rage in 1968. My straight blond hair rested on my shoulders and my skinny body had finally found a few curves. Bill and I dated for two perfect months and he was my first lover. Then my parents insisted I go visit my grandfather in Las Vegas for the long-standing annual two-week visit. More likely it was an effort to end our relationship, but I agreed to go.

While I was gone, Bill crawled into the back of his van and overdosed. I met his mother once afterward. She was heartbroken and guilt-ridden. She kept saying, "I knew I should have checked the van sooner. Did he ever say anything to you?"

My parents called Grandpa who told me the news and brought me a glass of milk. Not long after returning home, I went to the cemetery to see Bill's grave. I was sitting on the grass when his best friend, Don, walked up the hill. He started to leave, changed his mind and joined me. I did not know him well but we sat in the cool breeze, gazing out over the valley. Don said the tiny stream, trickling close by, would make Bill crazy. We shared memories for a very long time, taking comfort in the telling. They grew up together but my time with Bill had been very short and I was just sad that I did not have more to offer. I never saw Don again but I heard he robbed a liquor store and was shooting up the hard stuff.

MOVING TO HAWAI'I, TAKE ONE

I was nineteen the first time I moved to Hawai'i, arriving in Waikīkī with two girlfriends, no job, no place to live and a couple hundred dollars in my pocket. We checked into a hotel with a free phone, bought the local paper, a little junk food and started dialing. In three days, we had rented studio apartments on Ka'iulani, located on the edge of what was then called "The Jungle" due to its unsafe reputation. Determined to live alone, my own studio was on the ground floor. The rooms were partially furnished with a kitchenette, two twin beds, a table, two chairs, linoleum floors, cinder block walls and high louvered windows at each end. I had brought sheets and towels from home. Who needed a pillow? We had arrived.

Conservative Leslie found a clerk position in the industrial area. Suzie, the wild one, headed straight for Waikīkī Beach, walked up to the biggest surfboard rental kiosk perched on the sand and talked her way into a job. Surrounded by surfers, she was in heaven. I was promptly employed by Don the Beachcomber at the International Market Place, selling souvenirs and jewelry from the open-air carts, making $1.60 per hour plus nominal commissions. I was the top seller and a competing cart offered me five cents more per hour. With two jobs, I worked eight to twelve hours, six days a week, and had fifty dollars left after paying rent

My friend Brad was a valet at the Red Vest Restaurant on Kūhiō Avenue. The clientele were believed to be local mafia. We sat on the low wall many tropical nights, talking under the palms. At the end of the night the kitchen tossed out the soup du jour. If we showed up with our own container, they filled it for us and sometimes added stale dinner rolls.

I learned to cook rice from the North Shore runaway beach boys. Between nine and twelve years old, skinny, dark-haired, brown boys with big smiles and sparkling eyes, they laughed easily and seemed worldlier than I. They rode the bus from their North Shore homes and spent the day in Waikīkī, unless they missed the last bus. If caught on the streets after eleven o'clock, they were held in "juvie" until their parents claimed them, assuming they had any. Sometimes they would show up at my door and ask to sleep on my floor. No pillows or sheets required, they just flopped down in their beach shorts and tank tops and went instantly to sleep.

They taught me how to make rice to stretch the soup: one knuckle rice, one knuckle water, cover, boil. We shared dinner, I told stories of California and they told me about rolling sailors, stealing things, dodging cops and life on the streets of Waikīkī. I asked why they never stole anything from me and they all laughed uproariously. Finally, one of the boys chided me and said in a matter-of-fact tone, "Because you don't have anything to steal." They became protective, wanted to meet my male friends and often scolded me for going to unsafe places.

I came home late one night and they were inside my studio. I stopped cold and asked how they had gotten in. They laughed and pointed at the louvered windows. "Easy," they said with grins. I scolded them but I was talking to air.

I fell in puppy love with a young man who took me sailing on his family's eighty-foot schooner. The boom almost knocked me into the ocean and I was never invited back. He dumped me for his high school sweetheart and left for California shortly after. Years later, I named my hamster after him. Brad moved to the North Shore. Suzie had her heart broken and went home. Leslie fell in love. My adventure had lasted six months. Broke and hungry, I returned to California for the next eight years.

LAYOVERS

The only safe thing is to take a chance.

—MIKE NICHOLS

LOS ANGELES

I returned to my parents' house in Pleasant Hill after my short jaunt in Hawai'i. I was twenty when I followed my new boyfriend, Bill, the accountant, to LA after dating for only a few months. He was gentlemanly, nice-looking and liked me. That was sufficient criteria to pack up and move to Van Nuys, despite having no job, no place to stay and no driver's license. Bill told me I could stay with him for a week while I found my own place. I thought that signified a meaningful relationship.

I hitched a ride from my brother and hopped a plane to LA. Bill met me at the airport with the local want ads under his arm. That first week, he drove me to the DMV for a driver's license, I bought a used Dodge Dart—which later threw a rod on the LA freeway because I thought oil was optional—and found a small apartment nearby. In ten days, I was independent.

I secured a receptionist job at Mark C. Bloom Tire, located at Sunset and Vine. It was a dingy upstairs office overlooking the tire bay. Mr. Bloom's tyrant of an assistant, Miss Hopkins, was tuned to his every need and was the only one that heard him pounding on the bathroom door, crying, "Hoppy! Hoppy!" when he locked himself in. They were both short, ancient and wore business suits. Miss H. had a wardrobe of colorful and artistic scarves. I was not allowed to talk to Mr. B. She said I was too loud. She was angry when the service repairmen flirted with me and then she complimented me on my competence at the switchboard when I gave notice.

After a year, still dating Bill, I was feeling quite mature, living on my own in LA. I flew back to the Bay Area for a family Christmas. This was back when you dressed up for flights. I wore nylons, low heels and a black miniskirt that flounced at the bottom, with a black long-sleeve blouse boasting the same flouncy wrists and a plunging V-neck. I had purchased a black push-up bra that needed additional assistance with four half-moon "poofs" that pushed my meager talent up to acceptably visual inclusion. I was quite charmingly sophisticated as I chatted with fellow travelers and reveled in my adultness. I enjoyed a lovely evening at my parents' house, happy not to be put in charge of the children's table. As I prepared for bed in my old room, with the green wooden dresser, oval mirror and tulip bedside lamps, I could not find three of my little poofs. They were not where I had left them. I looked everywhere, re-walked the house and checked the car. Nope, no poofs. Then, I had a vision of the lovely smiling me, walking along in the airport as a little poof fell out of my blouse, maybe as I left the plane, maybe at the luggage carousel or maybe I left a perky half-moon sitting on my airline seat. I missed those three little poofs!

I knew my independent LA adventure was ending when Bill did not come home one night. I stayed up worrying, ready to call the police. There were no cell phones in those days. He finally arrived home as the sun came up, fresh as a daisy. He grudgingly admitted there was another woman. I zipped my lip, walked away and called my parents. They drove their RV to LA, loaded up my acquired household, and home we went. They never said a word or asked a question.

AN ARTIST

There is always one you regret. Roger and I went to grade school together. I had a mini crush in intermediate. We attended different high schools, had diverse experiences and new infatuations. In 1972, at twenty-two, I returned from LA and enrolled at the junior college near my parents' house. Roger was in my geometry class; it began with study dates. I fell irrevocably in love.

Roger was an artist with long thin fingers, long dark hair and very long thin legs. I teased him about his chicken legs but he didn't think it was funny. He was a biker and that was when my motorcycle addiction began.

Flying up Taylor Boulevard, two dogs chased each other across our path. Unavoidable, we hit one dog with the bike frame, went down and rolled down the road. No leathers, no helmets. I was unhurt but Roger twisted his knee and later had surgery. The bike was badly scraped but undamaged. The dogs were long gone. We picked up the bike and rode home.

We spent many hours on long rides. As a biker chick, I had rights. I demanded a comfortable leather seat. I insisted the "sissy bar" be the right height and padded. I would lean back, center gravity on my hips and look up at the sky. I never needed to hold on, I was an extension of the bike, light as a feather. Occasionally I wrapped my arms tightly around Roger, his long braid pressed to my cheek, sharing our complete freedom as I savored perfection in our existence.

I asked him to paint me a mermaid. I was thinking of a svelte, rosy creature with a bright green tail. He painted a thin, long-limbed mermaid with straight black hair plastered to her back in ragged ropes, kneeling on the rocks, looking out on a stormy sea and angry gray skies, the sun a muddy yellow mist on the horizon. I loved that picture. I still have it. After our two years together, I wrote reams and reams of poems and heartfelt longings for him. He married five times. He should have married me.

A MYTH

My first love had killed himself, both LA Bill and Roger had dumped me for younger women and I quit junior college because I could not find a place to park. Single again at twenty-four, I went to a lot of bars. I was hunting. After one quick walk through, I could tell if the bar looked fruitful or not. If not, I left. In fifteen seconds, I could case a guy and decide if I would give him the next fifteen minutes. If he passed, I gave him my phone number. I remember a short guy who fell in love with me because we had the same birthday. I broke his heart right away, because for once, I could be the heartbreaker.

By now, I had no confidence in my ability to find a decent guy. I seemed to have a knack for relationships ending poorly and I could only think there had to be something wrong with me. I called a psychiatrist. Six months changed nothing until the day he videotaped our session. I forgot he was filming until he turned it off. I watched as he played the tape back.

"What do you think of the tape?" he asked.

I looked at him blankly, not sure where he was going with this.

"You know that's you, right?"

I looked at him like he was stupid. "No, it's not," I stated flatly.

"Are you sure?" he asked and raised an eyebrow.

I looked right at him, my tone emphatic. "Yes, I'm sure. That's not me."

He smiled. "Why not?"

"Well, she's really beautiful and happy." I did not see how he could miss this fact but he had sprung his trap.

He kept smiling. "Look at her blouse," he said.

I did.

"Now look at your blouse."

I looked down. It was the same blouse.

Amazement washed over me. That charming, laughing girl was *me*. I didn't recognize her. I was stunned and just stared at him. "Well?" he asked, one eyebrow still up.

"Oh my God. I *am* beautiful."

The therapist genuinely smiled. "Yes. Yes, you are."

That was our last session. I will never forget the moment I saw myself for the first time. I still went to bars and still rated guys in fifteen seconds. I was still the huntress but now I knew I was beautiful. And beauty has power.

THE CARPENTER

I met Christopher in a bar, of course. He was exceedingly handsome with a chiseled face, blond hair and blue eyes. I have no pictures of him. I cannot exactly remember his face. I never took the time to study the curve of his cheeks, the arch of his brow, the shape of his eyes. I only wanted to lean into his hard muscled body, his arms holding me. He was easygoing, thoughtful and always fell asleep after a couple of beers. It was not uncommon for a late-night call, "Hey, you want to sleep with a friend?" before one of us would hop in a Mustang or a truck to see the other.

It was so easy, no commitment. Then we spent more time together. He taught me to play parts of "Malagueña," a classical Spanish guitar piece and "House of the Rising Sun." When we went to parties, everyone wanted him to play. I sang "Summertime" for them.

I remember sitting in a kitchen with a friend, watching two young ladies circle Christopher, edging closer, constantly touching him. Sweet and guileless, Christopher charmed the ladies and, mistaking his openness, they thought they had captured him. When it was time to leave, I swept in, scooped him up and led him off as the young ladies looked on in dismay. He always came home with me.

I took him for granted. I cannot remember why I let him go. I tracked him down on one of my road trips. He was living with a nice woman and her child in a Northern California suburb. I called, he invited me over, introduced me to his girlfriend and offered me a place to stay for the night. He still had the afghan I had crocheted for him. He said his girlfriend hated it. When she went to work, I took him to bed. I regret I didn't ask him about the dark circles under his eyes or why he was so thin. Maybe I didn't really want to know.

ZOOKEEPER

Saints

During my bar hunting days, I managed a menagerie of critters. My brother Bert and I shared a charming two-bedroom vintage farmhouse on the outskirts of Concord, surrounded by distant orchards and encroaching houses. It had a single floor heater, an oval glass front door and a built-in china cabinet that displayed Bert's antique plate collection. We shared the house with a St. Bernard; a very opinionated, arrogant, perpetually pissed-off cat; three aquarium turtles; a house tortoise; a hamster named after a loser boyfriend and a housebroken baby goat. I never counted the mice.

Bert was always at work or sleeping at a current girlfriend's house. I kept up the homestead, fed our housemates and paraded a series of boyfriends through the house, confirming that the quality of men in California was never going to live up to my expectations.

Ludy, short for Ludwig, was my brother's pampered St. Bernard, born during Bert's college years in Colorado. Ludy was typical of his breed, complete with long white and brown hair you could stuff a pillow with and a marvelously soulful face. He slathered us with love in long, ropy drools that clung to our clothes in sparkling, silver permanence. He romped around the yard in thunderous bounds, played ball enthusiastically and knocked me over at every opportunity. He never complained or barked or cleaned up his own poop.

One day, our local Dairy Queen called, complaining that my two St. Bernards were hanging out and begging for ice cream and would I please come and get them immediately? I knew our one and only Ludy was safely lounging at home, but no self-respecting St. B. owner would ever abandon two stray Saints in distress. I called my brother and we met Chris and Daisy at the pickup window. They were both smaller than Ludy but every bit as magnificent. Obviously neglected, with matted hair, weepy eyes and a few minor wounds, they were dancing in place and drooling happily. One word from my brother and Chris wrapped his paws around Bert's shoulders and did his best to spread the proper amount of slobber on his face while Daisy danced around me, beat me with her tail and, as expected, knocked me over. Absolutely confident that we had come to take them home, they jumped into my Mustang convertible without hesitation.

We introduced them to Ludy, food and water. Bert hopped on the phone, canvasing veterinarians to find their owner using the names on their collars. The owners were located and the sad story unfolded.

The happy young couple had acquired the dogs early in their marriage and were very fond of them until The Baby came. Their world changed. It is a fact that newborns seldom encounter germs and thus the slobbering pair were banished to the backyard and sadly neglected. The reunion did not go well. We mentioned Ludy and the wife hesitantly and hopefully said, "Do you want to keep them?" Papers and all. Free. Bert and I looked at each other, and said, "Yes," together. A friend of Bert's wanted to give Chris a good home but Daisy had no suitors. She stayed with Ludy and me.

Around that time, Christopher of the Round Table, my big, sexy, blond-haired, blue-eyed carpenter made his appearance in my life. He and I took the dogs to the park for the first time. Ludy was well trained, had gentlemanly manners and enjoyed his controlled romp in the park, keeping clear of small children lest he break one. Daisy went on a leash that was tied around my waist, as she had not had the benefit of a disciplined upbringing. Daisy was dragging my five-foot-five, one-hundred-and-ten-pound self around joyfully, when she suddenly paused with that *Oh, my God, what is that!* look. She hop-stepped in place as I leaned back, bent my knees and prepared for the lunge.

I grossly underestimated our relative body masses.

She leaped and I flew forward, momentarily suspended in midair, before reversing directions and falling backward onto Christopher's broad chest. I regained my feet and Christopher released my anchor, a.k.a. the leash around my waist. Daisy stopped, turned, trotted back to me and apologized with her sad-happy face and generous slobbers for trying to kill me again.

Puss Face

Baby Cakes, who my brother promptly renamed Puss Face due to her stunningly bad attitude, was part Persian and part Siamese. She was a refugee from LA; she'd had a rough childhood.

At the cheating boyfriend's cottage, she was told she would be a house cat but then was tossed outside where she had to put up with a dumber than dirt Irish Setter whose brains had been bred out to achieve a smaller head. Once, the cheating boyfriend had tried to flush her down the toilet. She had kittens in the linen closet and someone stole them. Then I uprooted her, moved her to Northern California without a by-your-leave, left her at my parents' house with two cockapoos, a rabbit hutch full of guinea pigs and a free roaming tortoise.

She was not happy.

Puss Face and I reconciled when I moved in with my brother. The St. Bernards never came in the house and the other zoo mates were not obnoxious. She liked to sleep on the toaster. She never bothered with the hamster who was beneath her consideration.

I offered to board Christopher's sweet kitten until he moved into a new place. I brought the strange kitty home, set it down for an introduction and Puss Face spit, arched, hissed and glared. I explained that it was only temporary but got a tail in my face for an answer.

Puss Face, a.k.a. Pissed-Off Cat, promptly stalked into my bedroom and pissed on a pair of Levi's lying on the floor. She skulked under the bed and did not come out until the intruder left.

Circus

I found an ad in the paper for baby miniature goats. I called for directions and went to see the little wonders. I was alone, and not having anyone to talk me out of it, I acted on this bad idea.

There's a primal maternal gene that causes instant lactation (literally or figuratively) anytime a woman hears a baby cry. It can be human, a tiny kitten mew, a puppy squeak, a chirpy chick, a newborn horse whinny or a baby calf's stuttering call.

A kid goat's bleat is no less compelling. He walked toward me on spindly legs, an adorable little black and white baby with tiny narrow face, a perfect V shape in the middle of his forehead. He had oversized ears, wide almond eyes with long lashes, a button nose over thin pink lips that were slightly turned up in a smile. He butted my knees and gave another lactate-inducing, soulful bleat. I picked him up and held him close as he tucked his head under my chin and pressed his tiny gray nubs into my neck. His little back hoofs nestled into my hand. I was a goner. I gave the guy twenty bucks and put the sweetly bleating baby goat into my Mustang.

Back home, I locked my new roommate in the mudroom and went out for formula, bottles and nipples. Christopher arrived after work and I called my parents to come see my new surprise. I was so excited! I was warming a baby bottle in the kitchen. Mom's eyes got big and she clutched her throat. Dad's lips made a thin line, eyebrows furrowed in a horrified frown. He said, "Tell me you're not pregnant!" then glared at Christopher who looked surprised and took two steps back.

I looked at each of them just as my little guy, hiding under the table, gave a long, questioning bleat. "Where's my bottle?" he cried. I burst out laughing, swooped him up and said, "Here's my new baby! Surprise!" The relief on my parents' face was profound. Christopher regained his composure. My dad was disgruntled but relieved. He reached out and petted my little guy's knobby head. "He is kind of cute," he mumbled.

Circus was my best friend. He loved to jump up on the tall kitchen stool, all four feet perched close together, and offer dinner suggestions. In no time he was housebroken, made friends with Ludy and Daisy and totally alienated my neighbor with his 4:00 a.m. breakfast bleating. Sadly, meal service was somewhat contingent on the amount of alcohol I had consumed the night before.

On my days off, we often went joyriding. I put the Mustang top down, opened the side gate and two St. Bernards and a goat barreled out of the backyard. They could all leap higher than a tall building, so I let them fly over the doors. The Saints took possession of the back seat and Circus rode in the front with a leash to be sure he stayed put at a stoplight.

My life was full of Houdinis. Before long, all three of them figured out how to break out of the backyard. The SPCA, who knew me well by now, would call me to pick up my animals. The ten-dollar stray dog fine was not so bad, but the goat was livestock and his life was worth a lot more at seventy-five dollars a pop. My neighbor finally won the noise battle and I had to find Circus a new home. I put an ad in the paper and a man came to pick him up. To this day, I pray he really did want a pet and not a BBQ.

Desert Refugee

My grandfather often went four wheeling in the Mojave Desert. Occasionally, he would find desert tortoises that he mailed to my mom.

The first tortoise lived in her backyard and his hard, gray and brown shell blended into the ground cover. His rough, strong, scaly legs ranged all over the fenced and turtle-proofed yard. He turned up in the oddest places and might wander over as you lounged in a chair, just to say hello. He didn't have a name. There was a lot to graze on in the yard but he never failed to come to the back door when he was hungry for treats. He was patient and persistent as he waited for someone to come into view. He climbed up the one cement step, reached another six inches and scratched on the sliding glass door with his sharp little claws until someone noticed his funny tortoise face staring up in anticipation. Grapes were his favorite but he liked celery, cucumbers or any leafy green. When he was full, he trundled down the step and went about his business.

The second tortoise had the run of our house in Concord. He liked to hide in my brother's cluttered room or truck purposefully around the living room obstacles, unmindful of the other zoo residents and headed for whatever important turtle meeting he had planned. Nobody bothered him.

The tortoise studiously avoided my brother's stinky tennis shoes that seemed to live under the coffee table. Repeated requests to keep them in his own space were ignored. So, one day, I nailed them to the floor.

Houdini

My hamster was named after an ex-boyfriend. Arthur would often get out of his cage and disappear. I usually found him easily, but one day he had his big jailbreak and really went missing. I discovered a suspicious regurgitation and accused Puss Face, a.k.a. Pissed-Off Cat, but she, of course, denied all responsibility. My cuddly little brown and white fur ball's favorite hiding place was my brother's room, mostly since it had never been cleaned. Ever. The closet was a solid wall of "stuff" piled up to eye level, a perfect labyrinth of junk.

I was sure Arthur was a goner. A month later, my biker buddies were lounging in the living room drinking beer and someone casually commented, "A rat just ran into your brother's room." I jumped up and searched in every corner and pile with no luck.

Finally, I pulled out the bottom dresser drawer and there was Arthur, sitting up, paws tucked under his chin, nose twitching, little white buck teeth gleaming. I swear he was smiling at me as he sat in the "home sweet home" nest he had made from my brother's favorite mohair ski sweater. I was especially impressed with the dog food nuggets that he had purloined from the mudroom and stashed in the corners.

A TRAGIC BIKER

He was a black-haired, blue-eyed Irishman who kept his Harley Sportster in the kitchen. A thick braid of midnight hair fell to his waist and he was made of long, thin angles. He had killed the love of his life when he hit a grease spill on an overpass, slammed into the railing and pitched his one true love over the side.

The black Irishman fell a long, long way himself, and every woman wanted to save him. He only wanted to suffer. Lucky for me, he picked someone else to walk beside him on his road to hell. But I was the first girl he let ride on his bike after the accident.

His name was Roderick. Not Rod, not Rodney. Roderick. It was an Irish thing. His estranged father made gravestones. He never talked about his mother but he had a deep respect for women. A dirt road in a rural area of the California East Bay led to his home, an old one-bedroom farmhouse; the surrounding fields were unkempt and overgrown. He handed me a .22 pistol and we shot empty beer cans (there were a lot them) off a tree stump in his backyard. He said a woman needed to know how to defend herself. My black Irish lover had been born in the wrong era.

There was a dilapidated barn but it was not good enough for the Harley. If he had ridden a horse instead of a Harley, the horse's head would have been hanging over the kitchen's Dutch door, watching us drink beer, chase salty tequila shots with lime, smoke pot and hang out between bike runs. We never ate in that kitchen.

A powerful motorcycle is the one thing a biker can control and it becomes an anchor; a center of gravity for their soul. They live for the next long ride with nothing between them and God. Once, we jumped the railroad tracks in front of a Hells Angels biker bar, speeding up as we approached the tracks and launched off the rise. I flew up off the seat and came back down when the bike landed on the back, then front wheels. It earned a recruitment offer from the Hells Angels head mama, which I gracefully declined.

The interlude lasted a few months. One day, Roderick turned off his phone. I never saw him again. Just like that, no scenes, no drama, no explanations, no apologies. Only silence.

For two weeks, I played Willie Nelson's *Red Headed Stranger* album, the "Blue Eyes Crying in the Rain" track, over and over at full volume. The neighbors must have hated me.

MY LIFE IS A ROAD ATLAS

In the summer of 1976, I was at loose ends. All my relationships had been disasters and then I foolishly set Christopher, my knight in shining armor, free. I decided to abandon the hopeless California male and strike out across the western plains in search of a meaningful relationship with a man worth keeping, or one that would keep me.

I ignored the advice of well-meaning friends and contemplated the Rand McNally US road map, plotting an escape with two hundred and fifty pages of freedom in an 11" x 15" road guide. I had friends or family in Southern California, Nevada, Arizona, Utah, Idaho and Oregon. It was time to check the oil and pack for a camping road trip: summer and winter clothes, a sleeping bag, cooler, flashlight, cutting board, knife, a cookpot (though what, in heaven's name, did I think I was going to cook on?), camp plates and utensils. On the feminine side, I packed kitchen towels, candles, matches, a pillow, books, my journal and pens. Gas was fifty cents a gallon and I had a Texaco credit card with no limit. I was brash, fearless and invincible. I was also headstrong and completely disillusioned. I quit my secretary job and hit the road to let the adventure unfold. I was confident that both adventure and safety nets would faithfully appear as needed. They always had.

THE GYPSY MEETS A ROUGHNECK

Who names their child Thorne? A mystery, he looked like a Greek god: tall, muscular, sandy blond hair, long on the top and straight as pins. He was fair skinned with light brown freckles and white, funny, awkward teeth that you wanted to trace with your tongue. His dream was to become a writer.

I don't remember how we met, but I remember the hundreds of miles that we put on my Mustang. There were long nights in a tent by the ocean. Thorne worked in the oil fields as a roughneck and liked girls in nothing but knee socks. I drove him to check on his mother. She had multiple sclerosis and lived on self-pity and baked potatoes from her wheelchair. She was a bitter woman and he was impatient with her whining. We only stayed an hour.

We followed work to the Ojai oil fields. Thorne's job was to make or break connections as a drill pipe was tripped in or out of the hole on drill rig platforms. It was hard work. We rented a motel room with a kitchenette by the week and I went in search of a job.

First stop, a bowling alley café. I wore my blue polyester slacks and matching dress jacket over a white frilly blouse. I looked more like a secretary than a waitress. The cook was a young, tall, string bean of a guy with red hair and freckles. I found out later he was on probation and had to keep his job or go back to jail. I never knew what his transgression was. He kept staring at me as he handed me the application through the kitchen pass-through. I filled it out and he barely read it. Just kept staring until he asked me if I could start tomorrow.

My only waitress experience was a summer job at seventeen. Lappert's Ice Cream Parlor opened in Walnut Creek and a dozen of us applied. I didn't think my short interview went well but to my surprise, I received a call to start work. When I arrived, the conversation was strange and stilted. It only took me a few minutes to figure out they had mixed up my application with another Kathy and they had no intention of hiring a girl with a limp. Too bad for them, I was determined to have that job. I watched them squirm and then punched in for my first shift. To their surprise, I was one of the better hires and outlasted most of the gals who had no clue how to earn while you learn. I made the highest tips every night. They eventually let me go due to "cutbacks." With this wealth of experience and fully confident, I took on the bowling alley café and, of course, I was running the place in two weeks.

The time came when washing Thorne's oil-soaked clothes at the Laundromat lost its romance and I began to get restless. Whatever connection we were seeking was missing. One day, while he was at work, I baked a cherry pie from scratch (he really loved pies), left it on the table with a goodbye note and drove away.

IDAHO COWBOYS

After traipsing through the oil fields, I headed north to Idaho where my mother's only brother was building his mountain cabin. At Uncle Rodney's insistence, I attended the Grange Hall dance where I met my Idaho cowboy.

Cowboys are so sweet and ever so sad. Every whiny country and western song you ever heard is true life. Cowboys live to be in love, have their hearts broken, drink a lot, wear a pink shirt, ride the rodeo, drive a truck and marry their horse. They look the best in tight Wranglers and cowboy boots, shirt optional. They should never be allowed to say more than, "Yes, ma'am," especially when their boots are comfortably placed under your bed.

The California Girl sisterhood had a certain reputation back then. I arrived at the Grange, with the appropriate physical attributes and he sidled up right away. He was twenty-four, handsome and charming with a big cowboy smile. His daddy owned a huge ranch. He drove a Jimmy C truck and worked on snowmobiles and other vehicles that could kill you. We danced and flirted all evening.

I stopped by his workplace the next morning and he declared that I was the most beautiful girl he had ever seen. We agreed to a café dinner and afterward went back to his trailer for a beer. Cowboys know that a nightcap is what your granny wears to bed. A beer after dinner is an invitation. Sitting at his picnic table on the cement slab, he felt compelled to show me a picture of his sweet young wife and his two beautiful little children, whom he had left. Sometime between the third and fourth beer, he owned up to also having a steady girlfriend who was a cop.

I was perturbed; I never dated married men. I felt like I was caught in a warped Garth Brooks song rewrite and the only way out was to take him to bed and break his heart.

Trailer walls are thin and I could have sworn I heard a noise outside but cowboys are always enthusiastic so I kept my focus. And then I broke his penis. I'm not sure how it happened but I guess if you break a blood vessel everything turns purple, swells up oddly and looks very bad. I am not making this up. My poor cowboy was distressed that his most important family member was in danger of gangrene so we called it a night.

I saw him briefly the next day, on my way out of town. He confessed (cowboys *always* confess) that it was his police officer girlfriend sneaking around outside the night before, listening at the window and getting her heart broken by his double infidelity. It was all I could do to keep a straight face but I decided it would be prudent to make a rapid retreat before I got into a tangle with the law.

It was time to head back to Concord and the zoo. A few months later, I received a letter from his police girlfriend who thanked me for getting them back together. Well, I did give him back, albeit used and slightly damaged. It was all part of a country-western song, yet to be written.

. . .

I returned to my bar hopping days. The quality of men in California was still sadly lacking and the latest nameless boyfriend was the last straw. I could see the way California was headed. It was time for me to be my own Houdini and disappear. I began planning my exodus to Hawai'i. I packed household necessities in numbered boxes, labeled them with contents, ready for shipping as needed. I gave the zoo to my brother, sold everything else and gave my parents custody of my Mustang. I bought a one-way ticket to Hawai'i.

WHERE'S THE USER MANUAL?

Life is the art of drawing without an eraser.

—John W. Gardner

I MARRIED THE BOSS

I married the married boss. But in my defense, I didn't know he was married at first.

I arrived in Lahaina, Maui, in February 1977 with no job, no place to stay and no plan—as usual. I had done this before. I made my way to Lahaina Harbor, strolling past the tour boats, each with their own boarding platforms, overhead signs and commissioned sales hawkers.

The *Viajero* was a sixty-seven-foot, ketch-rigged, motor sailer. The boat's hawker asked where I was staying. "Nowhere," I answered, and he offered the company's office front porch, where, apparently, he resided. As the sun was setting on my options, I accepted but made it clear I would be on the opposite side of the porch.

As I was falling asleep, someone ascended the stairs, stepped over me, unlocked the door and went inside. My benefactor said, "Don't worry, that's just my boss. He knows I sleep here." The next day I found a room with a private bath and a shared kitchen. Wandering back to the harbor, a *Viajero* deckhand called out, "Hey, little girl, do you want to go to Lāna'i tomorrow?"

"Really?" I asked, excited.

"Yep, just be here tomorrow morning at seven." He was a nice-looking young lecher and I was all for adventure.

The next morning, he escorted me to the boat's wheelhouse overlooking the dock. He said, "See that guy in the white shorts?"

I nodded.

"Stay below the window. He's the owner and it's okay if I bring you but we don't need him to see you." I nodded and laughed, sneaking another peek at the dock. In my mind, I weighed the two: *Deckhand, owner. Deckhand, owner.*

They loaded their supplies and paying passengers, then the crew cast off and we were headed across the channel to Mānele Harbor. It was a lovely, calm day. Hulopo'e Bay was an expansive crescent of white sand and blue ocean. We barbecued half-pound hamburgers on the now famous beach and enjoyed a happy hour sail home. The question of deckhand versus owner kept running through my mind.

Shortly after, I met the owner. He was tall, attractive and subtle in his casual non-dating approach. He invited me on a supply run to the island's other side. We connected during the forty-five-minute drive and subsequently spent several casual, flirtatious days together. After all, I had slept on his front porch and stolen a ride on his boat.

A short time later, he celebrated his thirty-fifth birthday with the crew. I was one of two pretty ladies draped on each arm as he got totally wasted. The next day, I overheard someone ask if he had found his wallet. "Yes, my wife picked it up." I stood there, processing. Wife? Wife? I cornered Ingrid, a deckhand I could trust to tell me the truth.

"Is the owner married?" I asked.

"Oh, yeah, he is. But it doesn't mean anything." She was nonchalant.

"What does that mean?" I asked. She just shrugged and replied that he went out with lots of women and not to worry. What was I supposed to do with that? I had one cardinal rule: I never dated married men. He did not wear a wedding ring and he had lied by omission. I promptly took a break from our relationship.

A month later, he packed up his wife and son, flew them to Seattle, bought her a camper, pointed her to the Calgary Stampede and then on to her home state of New York. Upon his return, he professed to be single and our whirlwind courtship of travel, fine wines, candlelight dinners and nude beaches began. I worked in the office and we moved in together. That was how it went for a couple of years. Then, I saw thirty on the horizon and I panicked. Which is how I came to invite him to our wedding.

. . .

Caught up in a ticking biological clock of dismay, I began dropping not-so-subtle hints. I waited a couple of months, but no proposal. I tried a ten-day California retreat; surely, I would be sorely missed. When I came back, he had partied the entire time and gave me crabs as a welcome home present. That did not go over well.

Thirty-one was looming. In desperation, I told him I would get pregnant, leave and he would never see his child. Dirty pool, but still no proposal. I took matters into my own hands. I dragged him around to possible wedding venues, talked about receptions and cakes, shared a few invitation samples. I talked about where we should buy a house. Like the flu, I exposed him to every aspect of weddings and marriage.

"We" selected a little Hawaiian coral and limestone church, Kaulanapueo, built in Huelo in 1853. It sat on an open grassy point overlooking an expansive blue ocean. I set the date, ordered invitations, mailed them to friends and family, then handed one to the alleged groom and waited to see if he would show up.

I purchased my wedding dress at the only wedding shop I could find on a whirlwind trip to O'ahu. When I found the perfect dress, I said, "I'll take it." The salesperson, appalled, explained that custom-made gowns were ordered and shipped from the mainland months in advance. My choice was a used fitting sample. Undaunted, I explained my wedding was ten days away and they had to sell it to me off the rack. I chose a sassy lace hat, reminiscent of my cowgirl days, refused a veil and carried my successful purchases out the door. It gave new meaning to "something old, something new."

On the morning of our wedding day, I called my brother Bert to make sure the groom had not mystically disappeared.

"Hi, Bert. Where is he?"

"What's it to ya?" he asked.

"No, seriously, where is he?"

"Why do you want to know?" Big brothers can be so obnoxious.

Slightly panicked, my voice went two octaves up. "Tell me where he is!"

"Well, if you must know, he's in the bathroom drinkin' a beer."

"Oh." A pause. "Is he coming to the wedding?"

"You'll find out when you get there," he said and hung up.

I rode to the church with my younger brother, Kenny. The wedding party ladies had congregated in the bride's room that also served as the church social hall and cafeteria. There wasn't a single mirror so I had to trust my mother's assurances that I was a beautiful bride.

Kenny reappeared to assure me that the groom had indeed arrived. I gave a huge sigh of relief, which made the back of my wedding dress open wide with a loud whirring *zziiiipppp*. The hysteria decibels climbed until Kenny yelled at all the ladies to get out. He walked over to me, calmly turned me around and simply re-zipped the self-healing zipper. He let the ladies back in and left for the church.

We had rented a lovely six-bedroom house, with a pool, for the reception. Five days before the wedding, I had not ordered a cake or made any arrangements for a reception beyond giving the catering kitchen the task of providing food. I called my wonderful housekeeper, Ione, and asked if she could be there when the food arrived and make sure it was set out properly. She arrived at the house early and was alarmed at my lack of preparation. During the ceremony, sixty miles away, she set up a wedding party table for fourteen, complete with her own elegant linen, china, silverware and crystal champagne glasses. She directed the kitchen staff, managed the entertainers (who sang regularly on our dinner cruise) and purchased a guest book and pen. I don't know how the wedding cake appeared. My mother had brought printed napkins, matchbooks and favors.

Our first dance was "Blue Eyes Crying in the Rain." It was prophetic. I believed I had married a wealthy tour boat operator. Imagine my surprise when I discovered we had spent all his money on our courtship. Thirty years, numerous business adventures and seven children later, I invited him to leave.

VALENTINE

The oldest child was gifted to me when I married his father. I was too young and naive to realize the treasure I was given. Neither he nor my new marriage came with a manual. It was a roller coaster of mistakes and successes.

At ten years old, he sprang fully formed from Zeus's head and became a part of my life. After the first clueless year, I said to hell with the missing instructions. He was more precious because, even though he was not my birth child, he was my son.

On Valentine's Day in 1998, he made me a four-foot-tall red heart, mounted on a stand, with MOM, cut out in a big circus font, surrounded by a scattered bouquet of live flowers glued to the heart. I took a picture so it would always be with me. The flowers eventually fell off, but I kept it for twenty years until I cleaned out the attic and there it was. I sent Adam the picture so he would remember how much I love him.

The first time he called me Mom, we were hosting a political fundraiser. All the kids were required to make an appearance, hang out a bit and then were free to go. They lined up for the obligatory goodbye.

Each one gave us a kiss or a hug as they made their way out the door.

Adam was last. He leaned in, kissed my cheek and said, "Bye, Mom." Just like the six before him. I watched him usher his siblings along as I cherished the moment. Years later, he told me I was often more his mom than his birth mom. It was not uncommon for the title to be interchangeable. "Hey, Mom, I am going to spend Thanksgiving with my mom this year." What a gift!

IN ORDER OF APPEARANCE

Chuck and I successfully raised seven children to be decent and imperfect human beings.

In 1987 Adam was a senior in high school. He loved to play with "the babies," as we called them, and often kept them busy while I prepared dinner. One of my fondest memories of those early days was Adam lying on his back in the middle of the living room floor, his feet up, flat toward the ceiling, playing "airplane." Five-year-old Cinnamon was on one foot and Kawehi, at four years, on the other. Both were balanced on their tummies, holding their arms out in flight. Adam held two-year-old Kaleo in one hand and baby Cayenne, less than a year old, in the other. Adam had them all flying in the air on their tummies, giggling away.

In May 1988, Adam graduated from high school and turned eighteen, Cinnamon had just finished first grade, Kawehi was starting kindergarten the next year, Kaleo was testing preschool and Cayenne turned one year old. We threw a *lūʻau* at the Old Lahaina Prison across the street from our house. There was a lot to celebrate!

The following September, as Cinnamon had been accepted at Hawai'i Preparatory Academy, we moved to Waimea on the Big Island. Adam went off to college and two years later, I gave birth, at home, to Kekoa. Kekai was born at home sixteen months later.

When we told Adam I was pregnant with Kekoa, he said, "I thought you guys were done with that." Apparently not.

. . .

My advice on having children: *Don't change your lifestyle for your children. Fit your children into your lifestyle.*

THREE CHILD-REARING MYTHS

Children Seldom Break If You Drop Them Gently

The first baby is like a fragile, sacred gift. I believe mothers will never be as in love with a child as they are with the first one. I certainly was and every precious moment and new experience was a cherished wonder. My first child never encountered a single germ for at least six months. When we traveled, we packed a stroller, playpen, one of those flimsy plastic baby seats, a small cooler and an overstuffed diaper bag that could handle any emergency that did not require a lifeboat. Car seats were not mandatory in the eighties but the small plastic carriers with adjustable wire stand were often used on the counter to feed a reclining baby. I set Cinnamon's fragile carrier on the front seat and began to back out of the driveway only to slam on the brakes as an invisible car whizzed past my bumper. Yep, you guessed it, the plastic carrier tilted forward and dumped the child, in slow motion, onto the floor of the Mustang. Terrified, I slammed into park and reached down for my little treasure who looked up at me with big wide eyes that seemed to say, "What the hell was that, Mom?"

The Wisdom of Pacifiers

I did not believe in pacifiers. The first birth child never saw one, but number two thought he should nurse 24/7. Out of desperation, and much against my better judgment, I bought a pacifier. I promptly dropped it in the driveway as I was getting out of the car. Using the five-second rule, I retrieved it quickly, swiped it twice across my jeans and stuffed it back in his mouth. Good enough. Early immunity techniques should be included in the user manual you never get. The next time the pacifier fell out of the car, I ran over it as we backed up. When I showed Kawehi the squashed pacifier, his face crumpled. I explained the situation but he did not understand a word and was not convinced.

Travel Lightly

Things changed after the second baby. The diaper bag got lighter, the playpen went in a closet, never to be seen again, and I purchased a classy maroon Buick Riviera convertible. Child number one got a legal car seat right after the rope-a-dope incident and I played musical car seats for the next ten years. The second and third car seats were installed in the back, the stroller stayed in the trunk and a dusty diaper bag lived under the front seat for emergencies. The babies loved to have the top down and it never occurred to me that speeding along at fifty-five might take their breath away. They laughed as their fine, blond hair blew around wildly. If they were cranky and screaming, I turned up the radio as the speakers were placed on either side, right by their little heads. They all grew up loving music.

The fourth car seat went in the front so Dad often rode his bike. By then, there was no stroller, no cooler and no diaper bag. I would toss two Pampers in my purse, grabbed an old cloth diaper for spit-ups and walked out the door. Seriously, raising children was not that complicated. One should not overthink it.

THE NINNY

I nursed all my children. In at least three cases, I became pregnant again when the current baby hit the seven-month deadline. That was the magic number. I was told when you get pregnant, while nursing, it changes the flavor of the milk. I often wondered if it went from vanilla to chocolate, or, in my case, champagne. Either way, that was the cue for the little tykes to give up the ninny. Their first baby food was always *poi* mixed with breast milk. Babies love it, it's very healthy and it eases them into real life. If seven months passed and I did not get pregnant, I explained the rules and fed them poi anyway. It was mostly a boy thing.

Kawehi was the needy one. Traumatized by his lost pacifier, he wanted to nurse around the clock. Consequently, he was chubby and "healthy."

Kaleo was a gentleman. He never fussed. He nursed politely and leisurely. His little hand reached up almost apologetically and rested on my breast. A kind and gentle old soul.

Kekoa had the same boob fixation. But he was not as concerned with my ninny once I took it back.

He was obsessed with burying his face in his nanny's abundant breasts. He just wanted to rest his cheek on them. All the time.

Kekai really didn't care either way. He was too busy researching his world.

I held Cinnamon, the firstborn, every moment, nursing or not.

Although there was no new pregnancy hot on her heels, Cayenne simply lost interest.

The girls were definitely easier than the boys!

ANT FARM

I unintentionally started an ant farm. I purchased a secondhand, wooden highchair with a tray that slid out when you squeezed the metal clamps underneath. My dad painted it bright blue with automotive paint. I made seat cushions, and hand painted teddy bears and balloons on the tray. In our small Lahaina cane house, it sat in the corner, blocked by a cupboard and wall on two sides with the kitchen table close against it.

I hated vacuuming more than anything in the world. A cursory sweep, every few days, was my maximum commitment to clean floors. Sometimes, I swept the debris into the corner hoping someone would chance by with the vacuum. Bread and cookie crumbs tended to multiply under that highchair. The ants, who lived under the house, found the bountiful feast and quickly recruited a conveyor belt of workers to carry off the loot. Those ants kept the floor cleaner than I would have. The highchair, which survived all six babies, continued to be the sole support of an entire ant colony for years. It still lives in the shed, sadly, supporting no one.

CENTIPEDES

In 1988 we moved to Waimea, on the Big Island. After living in Lahaina for twelve years, I was not prepared for Waimea fall weather. It would be a kindness to say our new house was a fixer-upper. I ordered carpeting for the cold cement floors and at the last minute added carpet on the wooden stairs to keep dirt from falling through the gaps into the laundry room below. The stairs made a left turn at the landing and continued up. Instead of posts, someone had stretched the curly, decorative aluminum frame from a screen door to fit the opening on one end of the landing. It kept children and small pets from falling off the landing as they ran down from the top flight and hopefully made the turn. I saw nothing wrong with this creative adaptation. With four kids under eight years old and only a twin mattress and old painting bench for furniture, we were getting along quite nicely while waiting for our container to arrive.

One chilly evening a child pointed frantically at the stairs. I looked up. A ten-inch centipede, fatter than a man's thumb, was slowly inching down the stairs. The recent termite tenting had made him sick, and he was looking for an exit. I was the only adult in the house. I did not panic, we had lots of centipedes in Lahaina. I shushed the children and calmly walked to the kitchen where I pulled out my father's meat cleaver. It is four inches wide and twelve inches long. It is one perfectly crafted stainless steel piece with no silly leather or plastic on the handle to mar its engraved beauty. It was meant for business. As a child, I remember watching my father process the winter game meat, whacking off the meatless leg of a deer and making short work of the various deer parts.

Grabbing a dustpan, a broom and the cleaver, I crept up the stairs in my bare feet. I set down the dustpan and held the broom ready in a defensive posture. Raising my right arm, I came down on that monster with a mighty swing. He was in two pieces, still wiggling, so, Lizzie Borden got in a couple more whacks, observed her handiwork until all motion stopped, then swept the parts into the dustpan for a trip to the toilet. Down he went, in pieces, destined for the cesspool. Nobody wanted to sleep on the floor that night so all five of us slept on my twin mattress that was, incidentally, also on the floor.

I MISPLACED THE BABY

There's a history of misplacing one's children in our family. These stories, once shared, are handed down at all gatherings for multiple generations. My great-aunt Esther, the oldest sister of my maternal "floozy" grandmother, had approximately thirteen live births. After one family event, Aunt Esther and her brood returned to their country farm, only to receive a call from her sister who asked if she had forgotten anything, like maybe the new baby she had left sleeping in the middle of the big master bed? On trips to town, the older children rode in the back of the truck. After one such trip, Aunt Esther did the usual head count and realized she was missing one of her boys. A sibling volunteered, "Oh, he fell out of the truck about three miles back." Sure enough, when her husband headed back down the road, there was the seven-year-old, trudging stoically along the dirt road.

I was fated to take after my great-aunt after my last child was born. One winter evening, while cooking dinner, my children were seated around the table doing homework. I suddenly looked up from the stove and counted heads. "Where's the baby?" I asked. No response. In a panicked voice I yelped, "CHILDREN! FIND THE BABY!" The kids jumped up and scattered, all except my oldest daughter who stood up slowly, placed a hand on her hip and said in disgust, "Mother, he's on your hip!"

Sure enough, there he was, comfortable in the cross-body shoulder sling that had held every baby's butt for the last ten years. Safely resting on my hip with my arm around him, his bright eyes smiled up at me. There had been a baby on my hip for so many years, I had forgotten he was there.

BOB'S YOUR UNCLE

"Uncle" Bob, a good friend and client, had fallen into his own marriage trap after he held my newborn Kawehi for the first time. His favorite picture was of my three-year-old daughter, Cinnamon, as she leaned against a wall, hand on hip, holding a glass of red wine with an "I dare you" look on her face.

Uncle Bob loved meeting each new child over the years. He would hug the girls, fist bump the boys and talk to them like adults. Kekai was a delightful skinny, pale, blond baby. Uncle Bob was thin, pale and blond. At their first meeting, Bob looked down at the little two-foot toddler in tank top and diapers. Their eyes locked and Kekai stretched both arms up as Bob lifted him for a long and profound hug. Little arms wrapped tight around Bob's neck, both with eyes closed, two souls in recognition and reunion. Bob finally opened his eyes and held the baby at arm's length to view my finale.

One beat, then two. Bob's smile faded as his eyebrows shot up, eyes wide. He exclaimed in astonishment, "He looks like me!" It was true. There was a long silence as I looked at my husband and he looked at me. Then we both shrugged and burst out laughing. "He does!" (He did! He wasn't!)

EARS AND ALL

I often said if I ever got an ugly one, I would quit having babies. I do hope my last child does not take that personally. He was actually quite splendid. Kekai was born in our king size *koa* bed upstairs. When he decided to enter the world, I gave him fifty-four minutes to do it. My water broke, I had a few contractions, I told the midwife it was time and there he was, a skinny little thing.

Studying each baby's face was my favorite pasttime. I watched Kekai a lot. One day, I looked at my husband and asked, "Do you think Kai looks a little like a monkey?" His father studied Kai's face, seriously pondering the question. He nodded and said, "Yes."

"Oh," I responded.

Kai had fabulous ears. They looked so *useful!* Like he could take off in flight at any moment, if only he could flap them. They were perfectly shaped, stuck out straight from his head, poised for functionality. Dumbo would be envious.

Being the thoughtless mother I was, I once suggested they were so perfect that we should have them surgically extended so he could really fly. My skinny boy was not only all ears, but also very thoughtful. I mean he *thought.* He observed, pondered and considered everything, including his ears.

Modeling school was required for all children. They were so photogenic; I was sure some great opportunity would sweep my children into fame and fortune. That didn't happen.

The modeling school set up a consultation with an ER doctor turned plastic surgeon in exchange for a referral fee. That's how they made money. My children were perfect but I felt obliged to at least interview for the tummy tuck. Kekai, along for the ride, was five. To divert the doc, I studied my skinny Kai in his aloha shirt, shorts, knobby knees, bowl-cut sun bleached hair, solemn face, his big, wide eyes taking in everything. And yes, those stupendous translucent ears like small pink headlights on either side of his head.

Kai stared back at us, and then panic flashed across his face. His eyes got bigger as he made the connection to surgically extended ears in the same room as a plastic surgeon. Faster than lightning, he covered both ears with his hands, momentarily frozen in place. Poor thing. Kai was having visions of himself a skinny Dumbo, blown away on random winds.

MELE

When Cayenne was ten, her dad and I were enjoying a glass of wine after dinner, when she wandered up, in her pajamas and asked, "Would you like me to sing *Lion King*?"

"Sure," we responded dutifully. To our amazement, she sang the entire score, in a beautiful voice, on key, from memory. We had no idea she could sing. Later the grade school music teacher told us she sang "On Top of Old Smokey" for the talent show, going up an octave on each verse. She sang in school choir, musicals and contests for the next fifteen years. A member of the state choir for four years, she was named best vocalist and won many awards.

Her a cappella was flawless and I took advantage of her talent shamelessly. During a chef cook-off competition, teams had to guess the entrée from hints. Chicago was famous for its steaks so I called her on my cell, hooked it to the sound system and had her sing "All That Jazz" from the musical. At Christmas I drug her around to every major hotel in Hawai'i where she sang Christmas carols to the sales and catering offices. "O Holy Night" always made everyone cry; it was truly that beautiful. One time she sang it in the middle of a Hawaiian Air holding room before our flight.

On one occasion, I took her and Kekai on a hotel sales call. They made a "flash" entrance with a rousing version of "Don't Stop Believin'" and harmonized out with "White Sandy Beach."

I volunteered her to sing "The Star-Spangled Banner" at numerous events; she hit that extra high note at the end, every time. At one *paniolo* event, however, she forgot the words. When her dad had his restaurant, she sang Christmas carols, table to table for tips. Her godmother was a beautiful singer on our dinner cruise boats when we lived in Lahaina. Dalena gave Cayenne her Hawaiian name, Kālena Kuʻulei, and I always believed she shared her own voice with Cayenne.

COLLEGE TRANSITIONS

I did not realize living in Waimea resulted in such a sheltered life for my children. It became apparent when Kaleo transitioned from sleepy Waimea to college at Hawai'i Pacific University on O'ahu in the fall of 2003.

During the college orientation tour, we visited the financial aid office to check options. The gentleman behind the desk rifled through papers, mumbling, "Athletic? Science? The choir needs a—" I interrupted him. "Did you say choir? Kaleo can sing."

"They need a bass singer and it has a 50 percent scholarship."

"Perfect," I said. "How do we apply?"

"Well, you would have to audition with the choir director—"

I interrupted. "Where can we find her?"

He hesitated. "Uh, normally there's a process."

"Well, we're only here for the day. Can we meet her? Kaleo can sing for her and we will know if we should pursue it or not."

"Let me see if I can reach her," he said dubiously. An hour later we met Mrs. Duprey in the choir hall.

A beautiful young woman, not quite sure how we arranged our interview, she plugged in the baby grand and with great trepidation, asked Kaleo to sing a few notes. Twenty minutes later, she was handing us forms and instructions to apply. In 2004, Kaleo, along with Mrs. Duprey's chorale and vocal ensemble, debuted at Carnegie Hall. That was my first child to perform there. Six years later, Kai sang at Carnegie Hall with the honors performance choir.

Leasing the Outrigger West in Waikīkī was HPU's solution for dorms. Two students shared a tiny hotel room with a microwave and a mini refrigerator. When school began, I took Kaleo to settle in and familiarized him with grocery store locations, bus routes, libraries and the beach. Finally, I asked him what he thought. "Mom, I have never seen so many good-looking chicks in one place in all my life." Well, as takeaways go, that was a pretty good one.

. . .

All the kids grew up listening to sixties and seventies music. Adam would pick a record, set down the needle and I would tell him exactly what album, which artist and the song, in the first five seconds. Kekai, at four, would stand on a chair in the living room and belt out "I Will Always Love You" at the top of his toddler voice. Kawehi's favorite was "Wake Me Up Before You Go-Go." He loved all the sappy songs and folk music. We visited him at Loyola Marymount in LA for his freshmen parents' weekend. Checking out his room, I saw the Time Life music collection of *The Folk Years.*

Surprised, I asked, "Hey, Kawehi, how did you get my CDs?"

"Those aren't yours, Mom. I bought them."

"You did? Why?"

"That's my comfort music, Mom. That's what I play when I get homesick."

And that is the gift of music.

. . .

Cinnamon sang alto but her most incredible talent was hula. She often placed first in solo events and her *hālau,* under one of Uncle George Na'ope's *kumu,* won many competitions. A tall thin *haole* girl with thick, dark blond hair past her waist, Uncle delighted in unexpectedly calling her up to dance. She was beautiful and her perfect, graceful, powerful dance would make people cry. I remember watching her play soccer in high school. Her long colt-like legs looked so fragile, I was sure they would not survive a season. But they were rock solid, strong and amazingly graceful. Her Hawaiian name, Kawai Lehua, was given to her by a hula dancer. In Hawai'i, often the name is not the only gift.

AND THEN LIFE CHANGES

Common sense and a sense of humor are the same thing,
moving at different speeds.
A sense of humor is just common sense, dancing.

—Clive James

ROMANTIC OR NOT

Not long after my fiftieth birthday, I was having a tough time. My normally smooth face, wide eyes and tight neck were relaxing into little lines, sags and future wattles, along with a relentlessly growing waistline. When I was young, I swore I would grow old gracefully and never have plastic surgery. Then gravity took a running jump at me and everything fell apart.

I returned from a week-long business trip. My husband and oldest son greeted me with excited grins, led me upstairs and stood outside the bathroom door. I warily opened it to discover the whole damn bathroom covered in mirrors. It was a fun house reflection of my real and perceived deficiencies bouncing around the room.

They were so proud of their surprise remodel; they could barely contain themselves. My horrified face did not reflect the expected excitement. Their faces changed from self-congratulatory grins to uncertainty to confusion, then finally to hurt disbelief. I felt like a total bitch.

Shortly after, my husband and I were standing in the shower, as long-married couples do, when he turned to me and put his arms around me. He looked into my eyes.

"You know, God really knows what he's doing," he said with a loving smile. He continued sagely, "Just about the time the body starts to fall apart, the eyes go bad too."

A romantic moment, however subjective.

MAKING KEKOA

May 26, 2014. No one wants to pick up that early morning phone call. The one that trashes your life plan, changes your world, and rewrites the journey forever.

When Kekoa, at twenty-four, crashed his motorcycle and sustained a traumatic brain injury (TBI), the ambulance drivers didn't think he would live. The best brain surgeon in Colorado Springs was waiting in the OR when they arrived. At first, no doctor would tell us if our son would survive. The initial prognosis was not good. His surgeon was cautious, telling us that every brain injury is different and no one can predict how things will turn out or what physical or mental disabilities will manifest.

I never doubted Koa would survive and regain his own original and unique identity. With complete confidence, I told his commanding officer that I would give him back to the Air Force in eighteen months, I just needed a little time. I ignored the pity in his eyes—it was irrelevant, because there was no other option. They cautioned me to lower my expectations. I had only one defiant response: *"You don't know me and you don't know my son."*

. . .

Date: May 28, 2014
To: Family and Friends
Subject: Update on Kekoa

Kekoa is in an excellent hospital with outstanding doctors. He is on life support and in a coma. He is deliberately sedated so his brain can heal. It is too soon to tell if the coma is induced by the doctors or a result of the injury or both. He has a severe head injury but no other known injuries besides a few nasty road rashes. It is too soon to tell anything but his eyes are responsive and he can move his right leg and arm. He is on a ventilator, has feeding, hydrating and draining tubes. Doctors are positive but cautious. He is a very strong young man with a will to always succeed. I believe he will win this challenge also. The support of his Colorado Springs 'Ohana is tremendous. There were twenty people in the "family room" at any given time yesterday and at least ten coming and going today. There are so many people who truly love this boy that you cannot imagine how many lives he has touched, each in a profound way. It is humbling. They tell their "Koa stories" and express their love and respect for him over and over. We have been offered twenty places to stay, hundreds of meals, whatever we need. They will do anything for Kekoa and his family. Please pass on whatever part of this email seems appropriate to those who ask.

KC

. . .

> *Being TBI is like being in a glass box. You know what you are looking at, but familiar things pass by and you can't remember their name or how they are connected. How do you know what is outside the box when you're confined in it? It feels like people keep throwing balls at you, but you can't see them.*
>
> —Kekoa

. . .

Date: August 6, 2014
To: Auntie Phyllis
Re: Thinking of You

The improvement is amazing. He can lift his left arm above his shoulder and move it sideways. He walked around the gym three times with a "walker." His speech therapist tested him today and he is definitely ahead of a week ago. She was very happy! Koa and I had a long conversation tonight, completely coherent, about his accident, his job and his progress. He asked for a notebook so he could write things down and something to read in the morning before his techs showed up. I gave him a *People* magazine and told him to read the article on why Taylor Swift cannot find true love. He said she should come and see him so he could help her out! He kept the magazine with him to read in the morning. Swelling is almost gone around his face. No bruising. Neck still stiff but he moves it around. It was a good day!

KC

. . .

Kekoa's determination and persistence rewrote his story. He has a tattoo on his ribs: *I don't find myself. I make who I am.* Case closed.

BROTHERS

Building Blocks

So long and thin, it seems impossible that his gangly young limbs have folded together in a cross-legged pose before the altar of his creation. Bony back, head tilted to one side as he carefully places a block on top of the tall, quivering tower.

After a considering glance, he selects the next shape to complement the edifice that is growing in front of him. He holds his breath, ribs taking rigid form like the art on the table. Sharp cheekbones, beautiful round eyes hidden behind soft brown strands, his lips pull thin and tight in concentration. The angular block walls, stark inclines and painted arches continue to form an intricate medieval edifice on the low table as knobby knees and sharp wooden angles are juxtaposed in overlapping positions. He leans toward the towers, intent.

A stealthy shadow enters the room, unnoticed by the builder. It creeps closer, controlled, on silent feet. The crouching shadow focuses, aims and fires. The blocks tilt and tumble, crashing down, scattering widely, leaving only a half tower intact.

The Great Cataclysm, as the shadow would henceforth be known, has struck.

The builder's head jerks up as he locks eyes with the still shadow. A heartbeat is measured and the room erupts in crows and curses; a laughing, flying shadow pursued by a vengeful, relentless crane.

The Crane and the Shadow

Time passes. The Crane goes to college and lives in a city by the ocean. The Shadow goes to a military academy and lives near a base in the mountains. He crashes his motorcycle and isn't quite the same. I have a picture of them standing on a street corner in the city. There is a red brick building behind them and a wily, brightly colored stone fish protrudes from the top corner of the landmark wall. The Shadow, formerly known as the Great Cataclysm, is a civilian now with an awkward walk and little stealth. The Crane is still tall and oh-so thin. His arm reaches protectively around the Shadow as their mother takes their picture on a city corner, a stone fish swimming in cloudy skies.

AN INTRODUCTION TO GRANDPARENTING

I was visiting my daughter and grandchild in Corvallis, Oregon, when my grandmother title came up. "Grandma" was not going to work for me. I had little experience or opportunity to hone any skills and I certainly was not a natural. My daughter agreed and told me "Nanna" had already been taken by her mother-in-law. That was a profound relief. Nanna reminded me of the big shaggy dog that nurtured Wendy, her forever nameless brothers, Peter Pan and the habitually lost boys.

We both rejected multiple suggestions. Exasperated, I finally exclaimed, "I don't care if you call me the Queen of England, I am *not* old enough to be a grandma!"

My daughter responded with a snicker. "Queenie it is," she said. I was secretly pleased.

My granddaughter, Scarlette, was about eighteen months old when I was tricked into taking her to a "play day." I had no idea what this was as I had raised seven children with a stream in the backyard, a neighborhood full of kids, no TV and a succession of tragic and amusing nannies. Play day, to me, meant you threw all the kids out of the house and told them to go play.

I placed the car seat behind the driver in my rented compact. Having spent my adult life sharing a car with family members well over six feet, I dropped my seat back, squishing her little legs and off we went.

When we arrived at our destination, I opened the car door, unbuckled the poor child and waited for her to climb out. I offered a hand; she pushed it away. I watched as she tried to pull her legs out from between the seats with no success. I offered again, she slapped my hand away with an adamant "No!" and continued to squirm her legs sideways. She wanted to do this herself. No problem. She struggled. The next effort to help received a scowl. I waited. After a few more attempts, she looked at me with a sad face of defeat.

"Do you want some help?" I asked. She nodded slightly. I couldn't resist. I stepped back, folded my arms and shook my head. Her eyes widened in surprise and then panic. I laughed, moved the front seat forward and she climbed out on her own.

The playroom was situated in the back of a children's department store. Little jackets were hung on short pegs at toddler height in the foyer. One of the mothers (they were so young!) smiled at me as she brought out a small vial of patchouli oil and rubbed it into both her hands and her child's while commiserating with the germs that were being lovingly annihilated. I was woefully unprepared. I had no scented oils or disinfectants. Not even a Kleenex to spit on for facial cleanups. We hurried into a huge room filled with tons of age-appropriate toys; games, puzzles, dolls, trucks, trikes, trains and every wondrous toy you could purchase in the store.

Little Scarlette went straight for her favorite cluster of toys and completely ignored me. Not sure if it had anything to do with the car seat episode, I looked around for a place to sit and to my dismay, realized there was not a single adult bench or chair in the room. The mothers and their little ones were sitting cross-legged on the floor. If I got down on that floor, I would be crawling for a rail or grasping a doorknob to pull myself back up. I have never done a squat in my life.

Mothers and daughters wore Birkenstocks, knee-high stockings, bulky skirts and layers of loose-fit peasant blouses, sweaters and vests embroidered with birds and tulips. The boys wore flannel shirts and overalls. Everyone had brown hair in various shades of mouse. The boys' hair covered brows, ears and necks. The girls had bangs, several versions of French braids and limp ribbons. All visible jewelry was silver. They looked like refugees from *Little House on the Prairie*. I expected Michael Landon to walk in the door any minute, sweep up a little girl in a pinafore and swing her around in the air. My low-heeled pumps, turtleneck sweater, designer jeans and jacket, gold diamond rings, drop earrings and engraved Hawaiian bracelets cast me in the role of the "saloon madam."

I scouted around and found a child's chair that had somehow escaped the back room. I parked it against the longest empty wall, my knees just inches from my chin and called my office to check in. I briefly described my situation and heard the office girls laughing and hooting in the background. I was more resigned than amused but determined to persevere. Little Scarlette ignored me except for an occasional glance to be sure I was still there.

An hour later, I was ready to escape with her when one of the mothers stood up and announced, "Snack time!" What? I had waited too long and was now caught in a stampeding herd of children and smiling, unhurried mothers making their way to the little back room where there was a low table surrounded by toddler-sized chairs. Little Scarlette knew the routine and plunked herself down. I had no choice but to join them unless I wanted to haul her out, kicking and screaming, before the treats appeared. The mothers sat on the floor while I perched like a rare bird of paradise on one of the little kid chairs.

Each mother opened soft-sided lunch pails and presented carrot sticks, celery with peanut butter, raisins, fruit and gluten-free pretzels to their young dependents. While little heads were bobbing and mouths chewing, several mothers noticed I was empty handed. Never saying a word, they graciously and silently shared with Little Scarlette who was oblivious that she had been slighted by the snack fairy.

Wondering if I could find any common ground, I noticed one pale mother give me a sideways glance before asking in a condescending tone, "Does Scarlette call you Grandma?" I finally realized why my title was so important. Snobby grandmother titles indicated one's placement in an invisible hierarchy, known only to these young women. "Grandma" was clearly an insult. Little Scarlette saved the day.

"That's Queenie," she loudly informed everyone with a smile.

I smiled, then shrugged and said, "I was never a very good mother and I am a worse grandmother, but I *am* Queenie."

Conversation stopped and eyes looked elsewhere. Little Scarlette finished her snack. I used the chair back to push myself up, took Scarlett's hand, smiled brightly and wished them all a warm aloha. Little Scarlette happily waved goodbye as we made our royal exit.

NOTE TO MY HOUSE SITTER

Oh dear! Forgot to warn you about Bobo, the cat. He complains all the time. Be sure to close the bedroom door at night. He is a terrible sleepover. The cat beds scattered around the living room are to keep him off the furniture. He hates cat beds. If his bowl is full and he is complaining, just stir the food around and he will think you did something. He has his own cat door and will come and go as he pleases. Don't pet him or he will think you should. If he likes you, he will bring a present that you won't like at all, usually left under the dining room table. He is a mighty hunter, an obnoxious roommate and a total whiner. He is twelve years old and set in his ways. He doesn't like me at all and is very clear about it. (I won't pet him because I am allergic to his dander.) He is the last legacy pet from my kids' childhood so he and I tolerate each other. With any luck he will come inside occasionally, complain loudly, twitch his tail indignantly and stomp off. No need to respond. That's the best you can hope for.

Bobo and I were comfortable roommates for a few more years. One night, he did not come home.

He had never missed a meal before so I was mildly concerned.

He showed up the next day with his head hunched in his shoulders, his usually well-groomed coat rumpled and dull. He usually yowled in my general direction and seldom cast a direct glance my way, but now he flopped on the floor and looked at me plaintively. It was time to visit the vet.

Old age had caught up with Bobo and he was failing. I had business out of town and could not stay. I asked my daughter to keep telling him I would be home in a couple of days, hoping he would hang on until I got back. He didn't. I cried. I made my daughter bury him in the weed patch near the stream so I could say goodbye when I got home. I miss him.

THE STREAM

The stream in my backyard changes constantly and I have spent little time on her efforts to attract my attention. Tall sharp green reeds grow thick along the edge. Gneiss and aged lava rocks form the bed. Many years ago, the children planted a Lāna'i pine tree on the other side of the stream. It first came to Maui in a pot on board the *Vida Mia,* a Christmas gift from Susumo Nishimura, our tour bus driver on Lāna'i. Later, it traveled across the 'Alenuihāhā Channel, on board the *Viajero,* finally finding its home above our stream in Waimea.

Unlike the sturdy willow tree that lived in a child's soul, the stream is elusive and ever changing. Sometimes it is bone dry, unable to hide the naked rocks and stranded debris. Often, she nurtures a tiny, dancing trickle and small ponds for tadpoles. Mostly she prays for rain to build swimming holes for the children. The stream is at her proudest when a flash flood, forty-five feet across, thunders down from the mountain and sweeps away the giant bufo toads that croak loud and long in the night.

The children would sit on the lawn in the rain and watch the water rise, listening for the roar of the flood until it burst into sight, rolling up and over the banks, muddy and foaming as it swept everything before its turbulent power.

It was easier to let the children chronicle the many moods of the stream as I let it go unnoticed, intent on life's other urgencies. Since the children have all gone, I occasionally step out and admire her lively or violent spirit; just so she knows I am keeping an eye her.

RANDOM REFLECTIONS

Common sense: I would pay a thousand dollars per ounce if I could only buy it and effectively dose a few people.

. . .

The most valuable lesson my mother taught me: Don't leave the kitchen drawers open while you are cooking. That way you never have to clean spills and crumbs out of them.

. . .

The local grocery store had a coupon for Cornish game hens. I only had one in the freezer so I needed to buy another one. One Thanksgiving, only my mom and I were home, no kids, no friends, but it was OK because we had Cornish game hens instead of a monster turkey we would never finish. On various holidays, two hens made a great celebration for us. Once I cooked four so we would have leftovers. I started to clip the coupon and remembered my mom passed away on Mother's Day last year. I guess one is enough now.

. . .

In my next life, I will be more mindful. I will look up and around more. I will focus on things around me and actually see them. I will look beyond the thoughts churning in my head. I will write down my memories so I don't lose them. I will be free spirited, less intense. I will be more patient and compassionate to the people I encounter and love. In the next life, I hope I gain wisdom at a much younger age, considering how long it took me to acquire any this time around.

. . .

Memories are how life teaches you when you are not looking.

STORIES

Always have one ready
You never know when it might
Save your life
Make someone laugh
Give a reason to someone
Who needs one
Hide a hurt
Cover awkwardness
Fill a silence
Sacrifice a Truth

ONE LAST DETAIL

That day in Price, Utah, December 1953. My uncle had borrowed our car for deer hunting. He returned it with a .22 rifle in a gun case, tucked under a blanket on the floor of the back seat. My mother left my brother and me in the car while she picked up my dad's Christmas present.

My brother jumped over the seat and the gun went off. I suddenly left my body. I remember sitting on the seat looking down at myself, dressed in a little striped T-shirt, wispy hair, my eyes closed, my mouth wide open. I was screaming.

A gap of time. In the emergency room, I left my body again, now looking for my parents. My mother was sitting upright in a chair, her face in her hands; my father stood behind her with his hands on her shoulders. They couldn't hear me no matter how loud I yelled.

I returned to my body. Then life happened.

ACKNOWLEDGMENTS

Mahalo to my children for providing me with so much raw material.

I love you all, each one for your own special uniqueness.

. . .

Adam — "Taco Tuesday!" At ten years old, he was a wedding present from my husband.

Cinnamon — Who tattooed stars on her freckles. My firstborn. My mother said she was payback for having to raise me. I love her all the more for that.

Kawehi — Often told people he was the firstborn and there had been a terrible mistake with the birth of his siblings.

Kaleo — "Gather them." The oldest and wisest soul, middle of the middle and least likely to disappear in a crowd.

Cayenne — "Do you want me to sing?" Earth Mother and gifted child of my heart.

Kekoa — "Look, it's a naked temple. You can see under its eaves…gasp." A delightful surprise and forever my hero.

Kekai — "I am lithe and I am fleeting." My proud finale; his siblings all gave him their extra smarts.

Born in Utah and raised in Northern California, Kathy Clarke lived on Maui for eleven years before moving to Hawai'i Island, her main residence for the past thirty-three years. Since 1980, Clarke has built a successful event and destination management career and is widely recognized in her industry. Always active in the community, she has lent support to many nonprofits by sharing her expertise and extending in-kind donations for events. Due to the COVID-19 pandemic, the Hawai'i visitor industry shutdown over the last two years has allowed her to begin writing her memoirs, causing some anxiety to her seven children.

www.ingramcontent.com/pod-product-compliance
Lightning Source LLC
Chambersburg PA
CBHW071835190726
48292CB00005B/1781

* 9 7 8 1 9 4 8 0 1 1 6 9 3 *